# ANIMAL FEET

David M. Schwartz *is an award-winning author of children's books, on a wide variety of topics, loved by children around the world.* Dwight Kuhn's *scientific expertise and artful eye work together with the camera to capture the awesome wonder of the natural world.*

**For a free color catalog describing Gareth Stevens Publishing's list of high-quality books and multimedia programs, call 1-800-542-2595 (USA) or 1-800-461-9120 (Canada). Gareth Stevens Publishing's Fax: (414) 225-0377.**

**Library of Congress Cataloging-in-Publication Data**

Schwartz, David M.
    Animal feet / by David M. Schwartz; photographs by Dwight Kuhn.
        p.  cm. — (Look once, look again)
    Includes bibliographical references and index.
    Summary: Describes the ways that some animals, such as ducks, caterpillars, geckos, flickers, and black bears, move from place to place.
    ISBN 0-8368-2577-2 (lib. bdg.)
    1. Foot—Juvenile literature.  2. Animal locomotion—Juvenile literature. [1. Foot.  2. Animal locomotion.]  I. Kuhn, Dwight, ill.  II. Title.  III. Series: Schwartz, David M.  Look once, look again.
    QL950.7.S38  2000
    573.7'9—dc21                                    99-048371

This North American edition first published in 2000 by
**Gareth Stevens Publishing**
1555 North RiverCenter Drive, Suite 201
Milwaukee, Wisconsin  53212  USA

First published in the United States in 1998 by Creative Teaching Press, Inc., P. O. Box 6017, Cypress, California, 90630-0017.

Text © 1998 by David M. Schwartz; photographs © 1998 by Dwight Kuhn. Additional end matter © 2000 by Gareth Stevens, Inc.

Printed in the United States of America

1 2 3 4 5 6 7 8 9 04 03 02 01 00

# ANIMAL FEET

by David M. Schwartz
photographs by Dwight Kuhn

A SPRINGBOARDS INTO
SCIENCE
SERIES

Gareth Stevens Publishing
MILWAUKEE

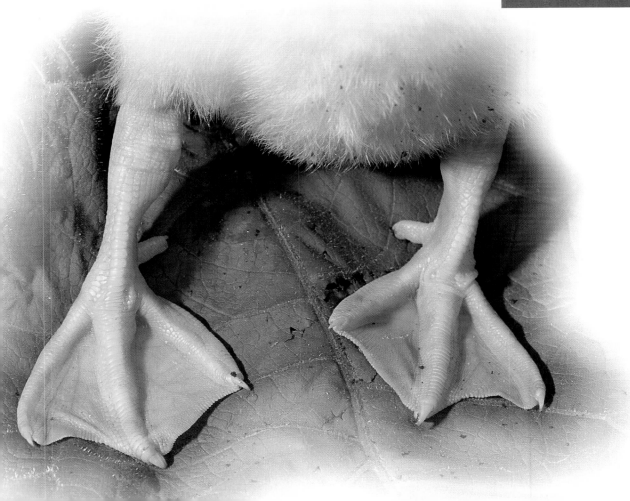

If you had feet like these, you could paddle across a pond.

5

Ducks paddle through water with their webbed feet.
A swimming duck may look like it is only floating.
Under water, however, its feet move quickly back
and forth. Some ducks also use their
feet to dive.

This creepie-crawlie uses its feet to move along as it munches leaves. One day, it will fly away!

Near the caterpillar's head are three pairs of legs. Farther back are flat, fleshy stumps called prolegs that help the caterpillar walk. Tiny hooks on the prolegs cling to objects.

This foot can go almost anywhere. So can the little lizard to which it belongs.

9

A gecko's toes have long ridges and sharp claws. The ridges contain tiny hooks that work like suction cups, allowing the gecko to grip onto almost anything. This is how geckos climb windows and walls.

This foot belongs to a bird that pecks on wood with its beak.

11

With its beak, a flicker (a type of woodpecker) pecks a hole in a tree to make a nest. Its sharp toes dig into the bark. The flicker eats ants and other insects on the ground, but it lives in the tree.

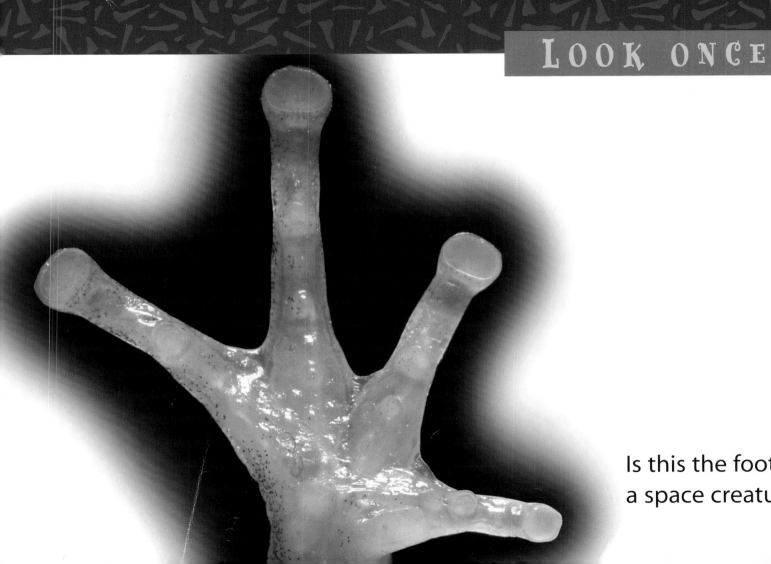

Is this the foot of a space creature?

No, it belongs to a tree frog. Little suction cups on its toes make the tree frog an expert climber. If you want to find a tree frog, don't just look in a pond — look in the trees!

These big feet
have sharp claws.

15

The black bear uses its sharp claws to climb trees and escape danger. The bear also digs for tasty roots and catches fish with its claws.

What creature has only one foot?

The snail! When it moves, a snail makes a layer of slime under its foot. Then, it can easily glide along its path.

**A.**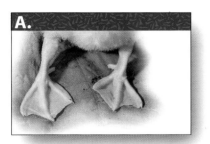

**B.**

**C.**

**D.**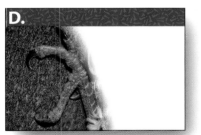

**E.**

**F.**

**G.**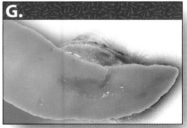

Look closely. Can you name the animals to which these feet belong?

# LOOK AGAIN

**A.**

Ducks

**B.**

Caterpillar

**C.**

Gecko

**D.**

Flicker

**E.**

Tree frog

**F.**

Black bear

**G.**

Snail

How many were you able to identify correctly?

**beak:** the jaws of a bird that have a hornlike covering; a bird's bill.

**caterpillar:** the wormlike beginning stage of a butterfly or moth.

**claws:** sharp, hooked nails on the foot of a bird or other animal.

**flicker:** a large member of the woodpecker family that has a brown back and a speckled underside.

**gecko:** a type of lizard that hunts for insects at night.

**lizard:** a reptile with a dry, scaly body covering.

**prolegs:** short, stubby, fleshy stumps on the abdomen segment of caterpillars.

**ridges:** a series of long crests or prominences on the body of an animal.

**roots:** the underground parts of plants. Some roots are edible.

**slime:** a mucous secretion from the bodies of various animals, including snails.

**snail:** a mollusk with a spiral shell and a broad foot. A mollusk is an invertebrate animal with a soft, unsegmented body that is usually housed in a shell.

**suction cups:** curved objects that have the ability to grip and hold onto flat surfaces.

**webbed:** containing a tissue or membrane that unites the toes of an animal, particularly many of the water birds.

### On the Trail

One of the main reasons an animal has feet is so it can move around in search of food. Tear a piece of bread into tiny pieces and dip the pieces in sugar water. Leave the pieces in a line on a sidewalk. Soon, ants and other insects will become aware of the morsels. They will travel toward the meal and carry it away! Be careful not to harm the little creatures.

### Footprint Find

To study the footprints of birds closely, you can collect their footprints. Sprinkle some flour into a shoebox lid. Shake the lid back and forth until the flour is flat and smooth. Place some birdseed in the center. Put the shoebox lid in a quiet place on the ground outside. Leave it for a few hours and then return to see if any birds have visited.

### Amazing Feet!

Make a simple bird feeder, and do some bird-watching. Smear peanut butter on a tree just outside your window. String some peanuts and hang them in the tree. Place some birdseed on a board on the ground. Notice the birds that are attracted. Do they cling to the tree with their feet, or do they prefer to land on a flat surface?

### Worms on the Move

Fill a jar with alternate 1-inch (2.5-centimeter) layers of moist soil and sand. When the jar is three-quarters full, gently place four worms onto the top. Place moist leaves over them. Then cover the jar with a dark cloth. After a few days, you will see that the worms have tunneled through the layers. How did they move? Do some research to find out if worms have feet. Return the worms safely to the wild.

## More Books to Read

*The Biggest and Littlest Animals.* Tony Palazzo (Lion)
*Birds. Young Scientist Concepts & Projects (series).* Jen Green (Gareth Stevens)
*Butterfly Magic for Kids. Animal Magic for Kids (series).* E. Jaediker Norsgaard (Gareth Stevens)
*How Animals Move. Animal Survival (series).* Michel Barré (Gareth Stevens)
*In Fields and Meadows.* Tessa Paul (Crabtree)
*The New Creepy Crawly Collection (series).* (Gareth Stevens)
*Wings, Stings, and Wriggly Things.* Martin Jenkins (Candlewick)

## Videos

*Animals Move in Many Ways.* (Phoenix/BFA)
*Just Ducky.* (Phoenix/BFA)
*Slowly Goes the Sloth.* (Bullfrog Films)

## Web Sites

www.kiddyhouse.com/Snails/
www.mesc.nbs.gov/butterfly/Butterfly.html

Some web sites stay current longer than others. For further web sites, use your search engines to locate the following topics: *caterpillars, feet, lizards, prolegs, snails, toes,* and *webbed feet.*

# INDEX